Christ's Call, Our Response

FOLLOW ME

JOHN MACARTHUR

COUNTRYMAN

Nashville, Tennessee

ACKNOWLEDGEMENTS

Martin Luther, *Luther's Works* • Roland Bainton, *Here I Stand*
Iain Murray, *D. Martyn Lloyd-Jones* • Iain Murray, *Jonathan Edwards*

Published by J. Countryman®, a division of
Thomas Nelson, Inc., Nashville, Tennessee 37214

Represented by the literary agency of Wolgemuth & Associates.

Photography: © istockphoto inc., © Getty Images, Inc., © Corbis,
© Anderson Thomas Design, Inc.

J. Countryman® is a trademark of Thomas Nelson Inc.

Represented by the literary agency of Wolgemuth & Associates.

Project Editor: Kathy Baker
Designed by Jade Novak and Abe Goolsby,
AndersonThomas Design, Inc., Nashville, Tennessee

ISBN 1-4041-0050-4

Printed and bound in the United States of America

www.thomasnelson.com • www.jcountryman.com

TABLE *of* CONTENTS

WHO CAN BE *a* DISCIPLE?

The Disciple's Resumé

Jesus' most intimate earthly relationships were with the twelve apostles, men who He personally selected and called to follow Him. From a distance, you might think that a friendship with the Lord of the universe would be reserved for uniquely gifted or strictly religious people.

But take a closer look. Those twelve were people just like you and me. They weren't distinguished for their natural talents or intellectual power. They were prone to mistakes, wrong attitudes, lapses of faith, and bitter failures. They came mainly from ordinary occupations that never would have suggested they were candidates for spiritual success.

Yet those ordinary men had an extraordinary relationship with the Master. They talked with Him. They walked with Him. They heard Him teach. They saw Him lay hands on the sick and raise the dead to new life. Eventually they heard Him call them "friends" (John 15:14–15). "Friends"—with God Himself!

Do you long for an intimate relationship with your God and Savior? Take heart—He delights in making Himself known to those with no earthly pedigree. He doesn't look for those with earthly accomplishments, but for those who have humble hearts and bow before the authority of His Word (Isaiah 66:2).

Does that describe you? If so, join me as we look at the lives of people who followed Christ—and some who didn't. In the process, you'll find the keys that unlock your own deeper walk with our wonderful, merciful Savior, the Lord Jesus Christ.

Disciple or Pretender?

Unusual events draw crowds like a magnet. I live in Southern California, and periodically we have spectacular wildfires that devastate homes and property for miles. The fires and the emergency equipment always attract curious crowds who welcome the opportunity to experience first-hand something extraordinary. But when the flames die out and the firemen finish their jobs, everyone goes back to what they had been doing. Superficial curiosity never sustains a crowd's interest for very long.

> HE DOESN'T LOOK FOR THOSE WITH EARTHLY ACCOMPLISHMENTS, BUT FOR THOSE WHO HAVE HUMBLE HEARTS AND BOW BEFORE THE AUTHORITY OF HIS WORD.

Jesus saw superficial curiosity in His

ministry. When word spread about His teaching and miracles, crowds gathered to hear Him speak and see Him perform miraculous healings (Matthew 4:24–25). Modern–day consultants might have advised Jesus to exploit His popularity and develop the broadest following possible by avoiding controversies that would have cut into the crowds' size. After all, isn't it better for people to be on the fringe than to be outside the ministry altogether?

But Jesus wasn't concerned with breaking attendance records. When the crowds reached their peak, He preached a confrontational message with such offensive content that the multitude melted away, leaving only a few devoted disciples behind (John 6:66–71). The crowd's superficial attraction to an unusual teacher didn't last. They ultimately didn't like His teaching. So they rejected the miracles and returned to their former ways of living.

But a few persisted. Why did they stay? Peter spoke for them when he said, "Lord, to whom shall we go? You have words of eternal life" (John 6:68). Peter followed the Lord even when Jesus had lost His popularity because he knew that Christ was the exclusive source of the teaching that leads to forgiveness of sins and eternal life. Peter valued those precious words more than being part of the crowd.

Do the prevailing opinions of those around you affect your enthusiasm for the Christian life? Or do you hunger and thirst after Christ regardless of what the next guy thinks? A true Christian follows even when the pretenders fall away.

Come—Just as You Are?

A catchy worship chorus is making the rounds with lyrics that invite you to "Come, just as you are, to worship." There's truth to that invitation if you understand it to mean that you cannot generate any human works to improve your standing with God and make yourself acceptable to Him.

But if those lyrics encourage someone to enter lightly into the presence of the Lord with no thought of self–examination or confession, a key biblical point will have been missed. The standard for approaching God is not "just as you are." In Matthew 5:48, Jesus said to all believers, "Be perfect, as your Father in heaven is perfect."

Frankly, no one meets that standard. Humanly speaking, no one qualifies when the standard is utter perfection. No one is fit to be in God's kingdom; no one is inherently worthy to be in God's presence. All have sinned and fall short of God's glory (Romans 3:23). There is none righteous, no, not one (Romans 3:10). Until the sinner recognizes that he is separated from God, true discipleship cannot take place at all.

There are no intrinsically qualified people to

No one is inherently qualified to serve as His disciple. God Himself must save sinners, sanctify them, and then transform them from the unqualified into the instruments He can use.

*Unless I am convicted
by Scripture and plain reason—
I do not accept the authority of
popes and councils, for they have
contradicted each other—
my conscience is captive to the
Word of God. I cannot and I will
not recant anything, for to go
against conscience is neither right
nor safe. Here I stand, I cannot do
otherwise. God help me. Amen.*

MARTIN LUTHER

come and worship God; no one is inherently qualified to serve as His disciple. God Himself must save sinners, sanctify them, and then transform them from the unqualified into the instruments He can use.

The starting point for discipleship is to recognize that you cannot follow Christ "just as you are." A change must take place inside you. You need to be born again (John 3:5) by repenting of your sins and believing in Christ as your Lord and Savior. Only then can you approach God with acceptable worship and follow Christ as a true disciple (John 14:6).

Crushed, Then Lifted Up, by God's Righteousness

In the sixteenth century, a German monk named Martin Luther sat in the tower of the Black Cloister in Wittenberg, meditating on the perfect righteousness of God. Although he was the most scrupulous of monks, attending confession for hours each day and seeking forgiveness for the smallest of sins, he realized that the standard of perfect righteousness was absolutely unattainable. Luther thought of divine righteousness as an unrelenting, unforgiving, avenging wrath, and he believed his state was hopeless.

But he found hope in Paul's words in Romans 1:16–17. Recounting the experience that transformed his life, he later said:

> That expression "righteousness of God" was like a thunderbolt in my heart. . . . I hated Paul with all my heart when I read that the righteousness of God is revealed in the gospel [Romans 1:16–17]. Only afterward, when I saw the words

that follow—namely, that it is written that the righteous shall live through faith [1:17]—and in addition consulted Augustine, I was cheered. When I learned that the righteousness of God is his mercy, and that he makes us righteous through it, a remedy was offered to me in my affliction (Martin Luther, *Luther's Works*, 54:308–9).

The remedy Luther found was the doctrine of justification by faith, a scriptural teaching that had been lost during the rise of the Roman Catholic Church. Luther's recovery of that doctrine launched the Reformation.

What Luther came to realize is that God's righteousness, revealed in the gospel, is reckoned in full to the account of everyone who turns to Christ in repentant faith. God's own righteousness thus becomes the ground on which believers stand before Him, and it becomes the foundation for a true walk with Him.

Here I Stand

After Martin Luther's writings began to circulate in the early 16th century, he quickly found himself embroiled in a life–and–death controversy due to opposition from the Roman Catholic Church. He ultimately faced charges of heresy in a trial before the very emperor of the so–called Holy Roman Empire, Charles V.

Luther knew full well that the trial could result in his death. As he contemplated the possible outcome of the trial, he wrote,

> If violence is used, as well it may be, I commend my cause
> to God. . . . My head is worth nothing compared with
> Christ. This is no time to think of safety. I must take care
> that the gospel is not brought into contempt by our fear to
> confess and seal our teaching with our blood (Roland
> Bainton, *Here I Stand*, 174).

At the climax of the trial, Luther was called upon to recant his beliefs and writings. Knowing full well that his earthly life hung in the balance, Luther was faithful to the Word of God.

> Unless I am convicted by Scripture and plain reason—I do
> not accept the authority of popes and councils, for they
> have contradicted each other—my conscience is captive to
> the Word of God. I cannot and I will not recant anything,
> for to go against conscience is neither right nor safe.
> Here I stand, I cannot do otherwise. God help me. Amen.
> (Ibid., 185).

Luther's indomitable courage fanned the flames of the Reformation, and the fire hasn't been doused since.

The challenges to your faith probably will be less dramatic than those Luther faced nearly five hundred years ago. But his heroic stand still beckons today's disciples to stand firm against those who would use intimidation to hinder the spread of the gospel of Christ. Luther calls us to remember that a man is never more noble than when he stands alone for Christ.

WHEN A
CHRISTIAN
MATURES IN HIS
WALK WITH THE
LORD, HE SEES
HIMSELF GETTING
SMALLER AND
SMALLER UNTIL,
LIKE THE MORNING
STAR, HE GIVES
WAY TO THE
RISING SUN.

When Less Is More

An old pastor once said he could always tell when a Christian was growing because a growing Christian would always talk more about Christ and less about himself. When a Christian matures in his walk with the Lord, he sees himself getting smaller and smaller until, like the morning star, he gives way to the rising sun.

John the Baptist illustrates that truth. God appointed John to prepare the way for Christ by proclaiming a baptism of repentance for the forgiveness of sins. His ministry was wildly successful. The Bible says all the country of Judea and all the people of Jerusalem were going out to hear him preach (Mark 1:4–5).

But John understood that his ministry wasn't designed to

attract attention to himself. He told the crowds, "After me One is coming who is mightier than I, and I am not fit to stoop down and untie the thong of His sandals" (Mark 1:7). "He must increase, but I must decrease" (John 3:30).

Whether you're a person of great or small stature in the eyes of the world, your life and resources have been given to you only so that you can reflect glory to the Lord Jesus Christ and make His praises known. Yield the spotlight to Him in your conversations today so that He can receive more of the glory He so richly deserves.

WHETHER YOU'RE A PERSON OF GREAT OR SMALL STATURE IN THE EYES OF THE WORLD, YOUR LIFE AND RESOURCES HAVE BEEN GIVEN TO YOU ONLY SO THAT YOU CAN REFLECT GLORY TO THE LORD JESUS CHRIST AND MAKE HIS PRAISES KNOWN.

The Emptiness of Wealth and Fame

Any informed list of the greatest evangelical preachers from the 20th century would certainly include Martyn Lloyd–Jones near the top. Even though he died in 1981, his books and tapes are still widely distributed today. I have personally benefited from his ministry for many years.

Some people are surprised to learn that Lloyd–Jones had risen to prominence as a medical doctor in London before he left the practice to enter full–time Christian ministry. His decision to leave medicine was not made lightly—he later said that it was a very great struggle to lay aside his attachment to a doctor's lifestyle.

In the midst of the struggle, Lloyd–Jones went to a theater performance with some friends. The glamour of the play, the theater, and the surrounding city sights left many enchanted with the evening. But a different kind of attraction captivated Lloyd–Jones' attention when he left the theater after the performance.

In his own words:

> A Salvation Army band came along playing some hymn tunes and I knew that these were my people. . . . I suppose I had enjoyed the play. [But] when I heard this band and the hymns I said, 'These are my people, these are the people I belong to, and I'm going to belong to them' (Iain Murray, *D. Martyn Lloyd–Jones: The First Forty Years*, 93).

On another occasion, Lloyd–Jones described the social outings that he shared with top medical professionals in London. "I used to hear the mutterings, the criticisms, and the jealousies. It sickened me." Lloyd–Jones' biographer states, "What he saw of life at 'the top' killed any ambition to get there" (Ibid., 94).

Martyn Lloyd–Jones saw through the emptiness of worldly glamour and attractions and valued more highly building the kingdom of God through the proclamation of His Word. Not every Christian needs to leave his secular employment to pursue Christian ministry, but every Christian should

recognize why that incident in Lloyd–Jones'
life affected him so deeply. The best joys of
this world are shallow and empty compared to
service to the King of kings. "It is better to be
humble in spirit with the lowly than to divide
the spoil with the proud" (Proverbs 16:19).

*The best joys of this world are
shallow and empty compared to
service to the King of kings.*

TYPES *of* DISCIPLES

Peter: The Perfect Imperfect Disciple

If you've ever wondered about the power of salvation and the enormous change it can work in the life of a man or woman like you, you need only to look at Peter. You've probably heard sermons that highlighted Peter's failures, impulsiveness, and overly active mouth. I like to refer to him as the apostle with the foot–shaped mouth. He certainly earned the title!

But if we walked away from the Scriptures and had only a negative, somewhat condescending attitude toward Peter, we would have missed what may be the Bible's most encouraging example of a man who followed Jesus. True, Peter had an ambivalent, vacillating, impulsive, unsubmissive personality. True, the Lord rebuked him with the words "Get behind Me, Satan!" (Matthew 16:23). True, Peter denied the Lord with curses before He was crucified (Matthew 26:69–75).

Yet God took Peter with his many faults and failures and shaped him into a rocklike leader—the greatest preacher among the apostles and in every sense the dominant figure in the first twelve chapters of Acts. Before you're too hard on Peter, remember that he was also the apostle who walked on water (Matthew 14:29), preached a sermon that God used to save three thousand souls (Acts 2:14–41), healed a lame beggar (Acts 3:1–10), and even raised a woman from the dead (Acts 9:36–42). Church history tells us that Peter ultimately was martyred for his faith—the ultimate triumph of his courageous faith.

What does that have to do with you? Only this—that the same God who overcame Peter's failures is the same God who can overcome your failures and use you as a mighty instrument for the building of His kingdom. God knows all your failures and weaknesses, but He is able to overcome them and perfect you so that you can fulfill the purpose for which He called you to Christ (Philippians 1:6). The life of Peter assures us that God can still use us despite our most bitter defeats.

God will use you differently from how He used Peter. The miracles that Peter performed were limited to the apostolic age to authenticate

GOD TOOK
A BUMBLING
FISHERMAN AND
TURNED HIM INTO
A POWERFUL
APOSTLE WHOSE
WITNESS ECHOES
THROUGH THE
CENTURIES AND
STILL AFFECTS US
TODAY.

the apostles' message. But He will use you nonetheless to be His witness and to accomplish the unique contribution that only you can make to further His purposes. God made you and saved you for His service, and He enables you to serve despite the faults that tend to discourage you.

In the pages that follow, we'll look at Peter's life from several perspectives and see how God took a bumbling fisherman and turned him into a powerful apostle whose witness echoes through the centuries and still affects us today. Are you ready to respond in faith?

The Value of Curiosity

There is an age–old debate about whether true leaders are born or made. Peter is a strong argument for the belief that leaders are born with certain innate gifts, but must also be properly shaped and made into true leaders.

Most of us have encountered children who ask question after question—wearying parents and other adults with a nonstop barrage of petty puzzlers. One mother told her talkative son, "It's time to be quiet now. My ears need a rest!" As exhausting as those childhood questions may be at times, they may represent the seeds of a future leader.

Peter illustrates that reality. An innate feature of his temperament was his inquisitiveness. In the Gospel accounts, Peter asks more questions than all the other apostles combined. It was usually Peter who asked the Lord to explain His difficult sayings (Matthew 15:15; Luke 12:41). It was Peter who asked how often he needed to forgive (Matthew 18:21). It was Peter who asked what reward the disciples would get for having left everything to follow Jesus (Matthew 19:27). It was Peter who asked about the withered fig tree (Mark 11:21). It was Peter who asked questions of the risen Christ (John 21:20–22).

Obviously, Peter always wanted to know more and to understand better. And that sort of inquisitiveness is a healthy feature of being a follower of Jesus—especially one who can eventually lead others to follow Him as well. Inquisitive people make good leaders. They are hungry to find answers. Knowledge is power. Whoever has the information has the advantage.

So if you want to be a growing disciple and even a good leader, be someone who asks the right questions and who genuinely looks for answers to the questions that matter. Learning is a foundational key to true discipleship.

The Disciple's Initiative

Another characteristic that marked Peter's life was initiative. A man who is wired for leadership will have drive, ambition, and energy. He must be the kind of person who makes things happen. Peter often charged right in where angels fear to tread.

In the Garden of Gethsemane, when Roman soldiers came to arrest Jesus, the Gospel writers say there was a "large crowd" armed with "swords and clubs" (Matthew 26:47; Mark 14:43; Luke 22:47). A typical Roman cohort consisted of six hundred soldiers, so in all likelihood there were hundreds of battle–ready Roman troops in and around the garden that night. The Jewish high priest and his personal staff would have been in front of the mob, because the high priest was the dignitary ordering Jesus' arrest.

Under those threatening circumstances, Peter pulled out his sword and took a swing at the head of Malchus, the servant of the high priest. Peter undoubtedly was trying to cut the man's head off. But Peter was a fisherman, not a swordsman. Malchus ducked, and his ear was severed. So Jesus "touched his ear and healed him" (Luke 22:51). Then he told Peter, "Put your sword back into its place, for all who take up the sword shall perish by the sword" (Matthew 26:52).

> HAVE YOU FALLEN DOWN IN YOUR WALK WITH THE LORD? HE HASN'T ABANDONED YOU.

Think about the incident. What did Peter think he was going to do against an entire detachment of Roman soldiers? Behead them all, one by one? Sometimes Peter's passion for taking the initiative caused him to overlook the obvious realities. But with all his brashness, Peter had the raw material from which God could make a leader. Better to work with a man like that than to try to motivate someone who is always passive and hesitant. As the familiar saying goes, it is easier to tone down a fanatic than to animate a corpse.

Peter was bold and decisive. He always wanted to move ahead.

He wanted to know what he didn't know. He was the first to ask questions and the first to try to answer questions. He was a man who always took the initiative, seized the moment, and charged ahead. That's a vital characteristic of all great leaders. Sometimes he had to take a step back, undo, retract, or be rebuked. But his constant willingness to grab the reins of opportunity marked him as a natural leader.

What opportunities lie before you today? Approach them decisively and trust the Lord to bless your initiative.

Discipleship on the Rebound

As we have seen, Peter experienced great things in his walk with the Lord. But he also failed at times, most notably when he denied the Lord three times just before His crucifixion (Matthew 26:69–75).

Peter's failures, however, did not ruin him or disqualify him from future ministry. The Lord recommissioned him after His resurrection. When Jesus confronted Peter about his unfaithfulness and lack of love, Peter affirmed his love for Christ three times (John 21:15–17). The Lord did not give up on Peter. He reassured him that he was still an apostle and commanded him to exercise faith and obedience—as Peter had done in the past—and to follow Him.

Have you fallen down in your walk with the Lord? He hasn't abandoned you—indeed, He will cleanse you and restore you in response to your sincere prayer of confession (1 John 1:9). You can bounce back and know the joy of following Him once again.

MOST PEOPLE
DO NOT COME TO
CHRIST AS AN
IMMEDIATE
RESPONSE TO A
SERMON THEY HEAR
IN A CROWDED
SETTING. THEY
COME TO CHRIST
BECAUSE OF THE
INFLUENCE OF AN
INDIVIDUAL.

Andrew: The Value of Individual People

One thing I have observed in all my years of ministry is that the most effective and important aspects of evangelism usually take place on an individual, personal level. Most people do not come to Christ as an immediate response to a sermon they hear in a crowded setting. They come to Christ because of the influence of an individual.

The apostle Andrew was such a man. He was known for bringing individuals to Christ. His first act after discovering Christ was to bring Peter to the Lord. At the feeding of the five thousand, it was Andrew who brought the boy with the loaves and fishes to Christ (John 6:8–9). When some Greeks wanted to see Jesus, Philip brought them to Andrew for help (John 12:20–22). That's the way Andrew usually seemed to minister: one–on–one. He understood the value of befriending just one person and bringing him to Christ.

Maybe you don't have leadership gifts or the ability to speak in front of large groups of people. That doesn't mean you can't have an effective evangelistic ministry. Be an Andrew to the people you know and introduce them to Christ. The Lord may use your quiet witness in ways you would never expect!

Lydia: A Woman of Hospitality

The book of Acts records the conversion of an often–over-looked woman named Lydia (Acts 16:14–15). She was a leading businesswoman in her day, being a wealthy seller of fabrics. When the apostle Paul came to her city and preached the gospel, the Lord opened Lydia's heart to respond in faith to Jesus Christ.

The glimpses we have of Lydia's Christian life illustrate one way that a woman can use her means and feminine touch to advance the gospel of Christ. After she was baptized, Lydia vigorously ministered hospitality to the Christian missionaries. She invited them into her home while they ministered the gospel (Acts 16:15). She opened her home for the infant church in her city to meet and find encouragement (Acts 16:40). Lydia instinctively practiced the kind of hospitality that Scripture repeatedly commands of all believers (Romans 12:13; Hebrews 13:1–2; 1 Peter 4:9).

If you're a woman of faith, know that your willingness to open your home and make your guests comfortable with your Christian kindness is a strategic means of advancing the kingdom of God. Whether you're providing a rest stop for Christian workers or a friendly coffee break to a discouraged young mother, you're providing a platform to proclaim the love of Christ in a most practical way that God will use greatly to His glory.

Mary: A Woman with the Right Attitude of Worship

History has tended to romanticize Mary, the earthly mother of Jesus. Artists have portrayed her with a halo around her head and a mystical expression on her face. The Roman Catholic Church has presented her as larger than life and attributed spiritual qualities to her that have no scriptural foundation. In reality, she was an ordinary young woman with an extraordinary faith that provides an example of true worship for today's Christians.

After the angel Gabriel announced to Mary that God's Son would be miraculously conceived in her virgin womb (Luke 1:26–38), Mary launched into what I like to call "the hymn of the Incarnation," traditionally known as the Magnificat (Luke 1:46–55). It is unquestionably the most magnificent psalm of worship in the New Testament, and it reveals the right attitude of worship, the right object of worship, and the right reasons for worship.

We'll glean from Mary's example in the next few pages, but she illustrates first of all that the right attitude of worship is internal. In verses 46–47, she exclaims, "My soul exalts the

Lord, and my spirit has rejoiced in God my Savior." The terms "soul" and "spirit" both refer to her internal state. Mary exhibited a spontaneous heart worship that was utterly consumed with the reality and wonder of God's person, and her lips merely expressed the overflow of what was in her heart.

Mary's words remind us that true worship is much more than being overwhelmed by impressive cathedral architecture and stained-glass windows, hearing uplifting music, or going through the motions of a church service. True worship involves the moral impulses and feelings of a humble heart, coming together in response to the Word of God in a crescendo of praise, and presented in thankful word and thought to the Lord.

Is that your attitude of worship?

Mary: A Woman with the Right Object of Worship

The object of Mary's praise and worship is obvious: "My soul exalts the Lord, and my spirit has rejoiced in God my Savior. . . . For the Mighty One has done great things for me; and holy is His name" (Luke 1:46–47; 49).

Mary worshiped God because she knew He is the only true object for our worship. But, just as important, Mary worshiped God because He was her Savior who promised to redeem her from her sin. Although Roman Catholics have tried to claim that Mary was sinless, she was no different from anyone else—she was a sinner in need of salvation (Romans 3:23). And so she rejoiced enthusiastically, because she knew that the same Son of God she would bear would

✦✧✦✧✦✧✦✧✦✧✦

*My soul exalts the Lord,
and my spirit has rejoiced in
God my Savior....
For the Mighty One has done
great things for me;
And holy is His name.
He has done mighty deeds
with His arm ...
He has given help to Israel
His servant, In remembrance of
His mercy ...*

MARY (LUKE 1:46-55)

✦✧✦✧✦✧✦✧✦✧✦

HE HAS FILLED
THE HUNGRY WITH
GOOD THINGS;
AND SENT AWAY
THE RICH
EMPTY-HANDED.

also redeem her from her sin.

Her worship was directed to her Lord and Savior. He alone is worthy—Jesus Christ the Lord.

Mary: A Woman with the Right Reasons for Worship

Mary expressed three basic motives for her fervent worship of God, all directly related to the truth of His salvation. First,

she recognized what God was doing for her. "He has had regard for the humble state of His bondslave . . . the Mighty One has done great things for me; and holy is His name" (Luke 1:48–49). Mary was amazed that a holy God would do such great things for her when she did not deserve it.

Mary then continued in her praise to God because of what He will do for others. "His mercy is upon generation after generation toward those who fear him" (Luke 1:50). Mary knew that God would shower His saving mercy on everyone who comes to Him with sincere awe and reverence. Mary worshiped Him because she knew that future generations of believers would fear the Lord.

Finally, Mary worshiped God because of what He has done in the past. "He has done mighty deeds with His arm; He has scattered those who were proud in the thoughts of their heart. He has brought down rulers from their thrones, and has exalted those who were humble. He has filled the hungry with good things; and sent away the rich empty–handed. He has given help to Israel His servant, in remembrance of His mercy" (Luke 1:51–55). Mary was thankful that God, in His sovereign wisdom, has continually reversed the world's social order. Worldly people have eventually been debased, but those who have sought God in repentance and faith have been lifted up.

GOD'S CONSISTENT RECORD OF FAITHFULNESS IN THE PAST SHOULD GIVE YOU SUPREME CONFIDENCE ABOUT THE WISDOM OF HIS FUTURE PLANS.

We should follow Mary's example and view God's redeeming actions as the reason we should worship Him. There will be times when you can't understand what He is doing or anticipate what He will do. But God's consistent record of faithfulness in the past should give you supreme confidence about the wisdom of His future plans. If the future is uncertain for you, don't wait to worship God until you see how everything works out. Worship Him now, before you see the results. You have every reason to do so.

James: Well-Directed Zeal

The apostle James never appears in any of the Gospels apart from his brother John. What little we know about James indicates that he had a fiery, vehement disposition. Jesus called them "sons of thunder." While the apostle Andrew was quietly bringing people to Jesus, James was wishing he could call down fire from heaven and destroy whole villages of people (see Luke 9:51 56). James was also the first apostle to be martyred (Acts 12:1–2), suggesting that he was not a passive or subtle man, but had a style that stirred things up and made deadly enemies very rapidly.

There is a legitimate place in spiritual leadership for people who have thunderous personalities. Elijah was that kind of character. Nehemiah was similarly passionate (Nehemiah 13:25). John the Baptist had a fiery temperament, too. James apparently was cut from similar fabric. He was outspoken, intense, and impatient with evildoers.

There is nothing inherently wrong with such zeal. But sometimes zeal can be less than righteous. Zeal apart from knowledge can be damning (Romans 10:2). Zeal without wisdom is dangerous. And zeal mixed with insensitivity is often cruel. Whenever zeal disintegrates into uncontrolled passion, it can be deadly.

Ultimately, James learned the proper balance. Church history tells us that the one who led James to the judgment seat was so moved by James' testimony that he himself became a Christian. As they were both being led away to execution, he begged James to forgive him. James said, "Peace be with thee," and kissed him before they were both beheaded. In the end, James was bringing people to Christ instead of itching to execute judgment.

If I have to choose between a man of passionate enthusiasm with a potential for failure or a cold compromiser, I'll take the man with passion every time. Such zeal must always be harnessed and tempered with love. But if it is surrendered to the control of the Holy Spirit and blended with patience and longsuffering, such zeal is a marvelous instrument in the hands of God.

The Greatness of Lowliness

The disciples hit one of their many low points when James and John came to Jesus with their notorious request for the chief thrones in the kingdom (Mark 10:35–45). Coming as it did on the heels of so many admonitions from Jesus about humility, the brothers' request showed amazing audacity. It reveals how utterly devoid of true humility they were.

There is nothing intrinsically wrong with ambition. James and John's desire to sit next to Jesus in the kingdom is understandable--who wouldn't desire that? The brothers' error was in desiring to obtain the position more than they desired to be worthy of such a position. Their ambition was untempered by humility. And Jesus repeatedly had made clear that the highest positions in the kingdom are reserved for the most humble saints on earth.

> THOSE WHO WANT TO BE GREAT MUST FIRST LEARN TO BE HUMBLE.

Those who want to be great must first learn to be humble. Christ Himself was the perfection of true humility (Philippians 2:5–8), and it was He who said, "Everyone who exalts himself will be humbled, and he who humbles himself will be exalted" (Luke 18:14).

If you want to be great in the kingdom of God, you must become the servant of all.

John: The Sectarian Truth-Seeker

When people think about the apostle John, they usually envision someone who was meek, mild, and effeminate, lying with his head on Jesus' shoulder and looking up at Him with a dove--eyed stare. But remember, he was one of the "Sons of Thunder." In fact, the only time John's name appears alone in the Gospels, he's angry because someone who wasn't one of the Twelve was casting out demons (Mark 9:38).

John was sectarian, narrow--minded, and intolerant, but those characteristics eventually turned into strengths because of his tremendous capacity for love. Someone who is loving but who has no strong convictions can become a disaster of compromise and sentimentality. John's convictions gave strength and structure to his love.

John leaned on Christ's chest not because he was weak and sentimental, but because he hungered for truth and had a deep affection for Christ. God took that intimate truth–seeker and used him to write large portions of the New Testament, thereby drawing other truth seekers into deep communion with the living Christ.

Jesus' Pattern of Humility

One of history's greatest acts of humility occurred at the Last Supper when Jesus was with His disciples on the night before His crucifixion. John records that Jesus "got up from supper, and laid aside His garments; and taking a towel, He girded Himself. Then He poured water into the basin and began to wash the disciples' feet, and to wipe them with the towel with which He was girded" (John 13:4–5).

Jesus' act was an expression of pure humility. Foot washing was a task typically given to the lowest slave. An attendant normally would be provided in a hired banquet room to wash guests' feet when they entered. Foot washing was necessary because of the dust, mud, and

JESUS' ACT WAS
AN EXPRESSION OF
PURE HUMILITY.

other filth one encountered as a pedestrian on the unpaved roads in and around Jerusalem. But evidently no servant was there to perform the task when Jesus and the disciples arrived at the Upper Room. So instead of humbling themselves to perform such a demeaning task for one another, the disciples simply left their feet unwashed.

Christ's gesture was both a touching act of self–abasement and a subtle rebuke to the disciples. Jesus Christ—the Eternal Son of God who will one day come to earth in triumphant glory to establish His kingdom—took the role of the lowest servant and gave us all a graphic lesson about humility and true holiness. In the process, He left behind a powerful message for you and me—no act is too low for the disciple of Christ to perform in His service.

Are you aware of some humble task that needs to be accomplished, but goes unfinished because no one wants to do it? Be like Jesus. Pick up a towel, and do that menial task to the glory of God.

Matthew: Reaching the Outcasts

In all likelihood, none of the twelve apostles was more notorious at the time of his calling than Matthew: he was a tax collector when Jesus called him. That is the last credential we might expect to see from a man who would become an apostle of Christ. In that day, tax collectors were the most despised people in Roman–occupied Israel. They were hated and vilified by all of Jewish society, because they bought tax franchises from the Roman emperor and then extorted money from the people of Israel to feed the Roman coffers and pad their own pockets. They often used thugs to strong–arm money out of people. Most tax collectors were despicable, vile, unprincipled scoundrels.

> NO ACT IS
> TOO LOW FOR
> THE DISCIPLE
> OF CHRIST
> TO PERFORM
> IN HIS SERVICE.

But Jesus had a place for Matthew. Matthew 9:9 catches the reader by surprise: "As Jesus went on from [Capernaum], He saw a man called Matthew sitting in the tax collector's booth; And He said to him, 'Follow Me.' And he got up and followed Him." Luke reveals that Matthew held an enormous banquet at his own house in Jesus' honor, and that he invited a large number of his fellow tax collectors and various other scoundrels and social outcasts to meet Jesus (Luke 5:27–32). He was so thrilled to have found the Messiah that he wanted to introduce Jesus to everyone he knew.

Of course, the people of the religious establishment were out-raged and scandalized. They wasted no time voicing their criticism to the disciples. But Jesus exposed their hypocrisy by saying sick people are the very ones who need a physician. He had not come to call the self–righteous, but sinners, to repentance. In other words, there was nothing He could do for the religious elite who insisted on keeping their pious veneer. But people like Matthew and his friends who were prepared to confess their sin could be forgiven and redeemed.

Has a life of sin left you or someone you know in the place of social rejection? Perhaps your life isn't a public scandal, but your conscience condemns you for sins that you know all too well even if others are unaware. The life of Matthew radiates bright hope into your life. The Lord often chooses the most despicable people of this world, redeems them, gives them new hearts, and uses them in remarkable ways.

Thomas: Overcoming Pessimism

One of the better-known apostles after Peter and John is Thomas. He is usually nicknamed "Doubting Thomas," but that may not be the most fitting label for him. He was a better man than popular lore would indicate.

It probably is fair to say, however, that Thomas was a somewhat negative person. He was a worrywart. He was like Winnie the Pooh's friend Eeyore the donkey who anticipates the worst all the time. Pessimism, rather than doubt per se, seems to have been Thomas' besetting sin.

That pessimism was on display when the other disciples first approached him with news about Jesus' resurrection. They were ecstatic because they had seen the Lord, but when they shared the good news with Thomas, he wasn't in the mood to be cheered up. He missed the Lord horribly and the thought of the resurrection seemed too good to be true. So he said to them, "Unless I see in His hands the imprint of the nails, and put my finger into the place of the nails, and put my hand into His side, I will not believe" (John 20:24–25).

It is because of that statement that he has been nicknamed "Doubting Thomas." But don't be too hard on him. The other disciples did not believe in the resurrection until they saw Jesus, either (Mark 16:9–11). So all the apostles were slow to believe. Before you tag Thomas with a negative label, though, reflect for a moment on his faith. Thomas had erred because he was more or less wired to be a pessimist. But it was actually the error of profound love. Thomas loved Christ and couldn't bear the thought of getting his hopes up about the resurrection.

> THE LORD OFTEN CHOOSES THE MOST DESPICABLE PEOPLE OF THIS WORLD, REDEEMS THEM, GIVES THEM NEW HEARTS, AND USES THEM IN REMARKABLE WAYS.

But Jesus understands our weaknesses (Hebrews 4:15), and He was amazingly gentle with Thomas. When He finally saw Thomas after the resurrection, He looked at him and said, "Reach your finger here, and look at My hands; and reach your hand here, and put it into My side. Do not be unbelieving, but believing" (John 20:27, NKJV).

In response, Thomas made what was probably the greatest statement ever to come from the lips of the apostles: "My Lord and my God!" (v. 28). Suddenly, Thomas' melancholy, moody tendencies were forever banished by the appearance of Jesus Christ. And at that moment, he was transformed into a great evangelist.

START LOOKING
BEYOND THE
MINUTIAE TO THE
ETERNAL CHRIST,
WHO CAN TAKE
EVEN YOUR WEAK
FAITH AND USE YOU
FOR HIS KINGDOM
PURPOSES.

Considerable ancient testimony suggests that Thomas carried the gospel as far as India. There are churches in south India whose roots are traceable to the beginning of the church age, and tradition says they were founded under the ministry of Thomas. The strongest traditions say he was martyred for his faith by being run through with a spear—a fitting form of martyrdom for one whose faith came of age when he saw the spear mark in his Master's side and for one who longed to be reunited with his Lord.

Do you get the picture? If God could use a moody pessimist like Thomas as a great instrument in the spread of the gospel, He can use you, too. God meets repentant sinners with grace, mercy, and forgiveness and transforms their lives into useful vessels that glorify Him. You—even you—are within the reach of His transforming grace.

Philip: The Christian Materialist

The apostle Philip was a man of practical, common-sense tendencies. He was methodical and overly analytical, with very little under-standing of the supernatural. He was a facts-and-figures guy, always responding to mere outward appearances on the human level. He missed some spiritual blessings as a result.

After Jesus had spent an entire day teaching and healing the diseases of a crowd of over five thousand men, evening approached and the crowd began to get hungry. Jesus turned to the apostle Philip and asked, "Where are we to buy bread, so that these may eat?" (John 6:5).

Philip should have answered, "Lord, You've done miracles all day long. You have the power to feed them if You want." But he flunked his spiritual exam. Even though he was in the presence of the Creator of all, he sadly reported that even six months' wages couldn't feed such a crowd (John 6:7).

Later, at the end of Jesus' earthly life, Philip asked to see the Father, even though for three years he had been gazing into the face of God Himself (John 14:8–9). Philip suffered from poor spiritual vision and weak faith. He was slow to understand, slow to trust, and slow to see beyond the immediate circumstances.

But that didn't keep Jesus from using him. Jesus took that halting man, and according to tradition, used him greatly in the spread of the early church. By most accounts, Philip was put to death by stoning in Asia Minor. But before his death, multitudes came to Christ under his preaching.

If you tend to see the obstacles in life and have trouble getting past the details, you have a bit of Philip in you. Start looking beyond the minutiae to the eternal Christ, who can take even your weak faith and use you for His kingdom purposes.

Nathanael: Overcoming Bigotry

Nathanael first heard about Jesus from his friend Philip, who told him, "We have found Him of whom Moses in the Law and also the Prophets wrote—Jesus of Nazareth, the son of Joseph" (John 1:45).

Philip obviously knew that such a description of Jesus would be meaningful to Nathanael, who was full of faith and a student of the Word of God. But his initial response to Philip reveals a flaw in his character: "Can any good thing come out of Nazareth?" (v. 46). Nathanael was from Cana, and apparently thought that the people of Cana were more refined than those from Nazareth. Nathanael was guilty of the sin of prejudice: an uncalled–for generalization based on feelings of superiority.

> NATHANAEL SHOWS US THAT THE LORD USES TRUTH-SEEKERS WHO ARE FULL OF FAITH AND UNDERSTANDING, OPEN, HONEST, AND MEDITATIVE— EVEN THOUGH THEY ARE FLAWED.

Happily, the Lord overcame Nathanael's prejudiced heart, and he proved exceptionally quick to believe in Jesus (vv. 47–51). Nathanael shows us that the Lord uses truth-seekers who are full of faith and understanding, open, honest, and meditative—even though they are flawed.

You may be a sensitive Christian who is painfully aware of your faults. Know that God meets you like He did Nathanael. He does not deal with you according to your sins (Psalm

103:10), but according to His gracious riches in Christ. Rejoice and be at peace!

James the Less: Celebrity and Obscurity

Walk through most supermarkets and you'll get an object lesson in America's fascination with celebrity. Magazines and tabloids blare forth all manner of the latest gossip on the private lives of public personalities. You would think that most people had better things to do than read tawdry details about the rich and famous, but the publishers are obviously selling to someone.

Against that celebrity mindset stands the life of James the son of Alphaeus, one of the apostles. The Bible tells us only his name, and in Mark 15:40 he is called "James the Less," which could be a reference to his stature, age, or influence. From the name "Alphaeus," it's possible that this James was Matthew's brother (Matthew 10:3; Mark 2:14) or perhaps a cousin of Jesus (John 19:25). If he was, he might have been tempted to use his family ties to throw his weight around a little—but we don't see him doing that. There's simply nothing in the biblical record to call attention to him.

James the son of Alphaeus reminds me of the nameless people mentioned in Hebrews 11:33–38, "of whom the world was not worthy." The world didn't deserve those silent, unknown soldiers of the faith. Their lack of celebrity kept them from the pages of history, but their names are written on the pages of the Lamb's book of life.

Once again, we see that the Lord uses ordinary people to accomplish extraordinary things. The vessel is not the issue; the Master is. James remains obscure from an earthly perspective, yet the Lord sovereignly chose him to be part of His inner circle. As a result, this James serves as a great rebuke to the modern superstar mentality. He is largely forgotten on earth, but he will receive a full reward in eternity (Mark 10:29–31).

> THE WORLD DIDN'T DESERVE THOSE SILENT, UNKNOWN SOLDIERS OF THE FAITH. THEIR LACK OF CELEBRITY KEPT THEM FROM THE PAGES OF HISTORY, BUT THEIR NAMES ARE WRITTEN ON THE PAGES OF THE LAMB'S BOOK OF LIFE.

Thaddaeus: A Teachable Spirit

Another apostle who is mostly shrouded in obscurity is Thaddaeus (Matthew 10:3). The Bible also calls him "Judas the son of James" (Luke 6:16; Acts 1:13) and "Judas (not Iscariot)" (John 14:22). Like most Jewish people, Thaddaeus was expecting the Messiah to set up His millennial kingdom immediately throughout the world. But as he grasped Jesus' teaching, he realized that he needed to change his thinking.

Jesus taught the apostles that He would manifest Himself only to those open to receiving Him (John 14:21). His earthly

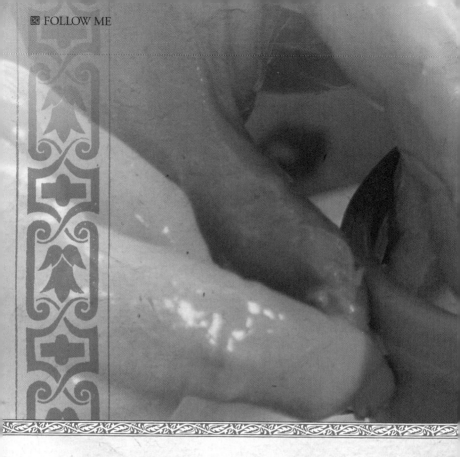

life was not going to result in the establishment of a world–wide kingdom. Most people would miss His coming altogether.

As the significance of the Lord's teaching dawned on him, Thaddaeus asked, "Lord, what then has happened that You are going to disclose Yourself to us and not to the world?" That brief question lays open the tender–hearted humility of this man. He couldn't believe that Jesus would manifest

TRUE SALVATION PRODUCES A TEACHABLE HEART IN THE BELIEVER. THE DESIRE TO LEARN AND CHANGE IN RESPONSE TO THE WORD OF GOD IS THE MARK OF A TRUE DISCIPLE OF CHRIST.

Himself to this rag–tag group of apostles, and not to the whole world. His question is full of gentleness and meekness and devoid of any sort of pride.

In short, Thaddaeus had a teachable spirit. He was willing to set aside his erroneous thinking so he could conform his mind to the teaching of His Savior. This pious, believing disciple loved his Lord and wanted to understand the mind of Christ.

No doubt he was encouraged by the Lord's tender, relational reply: "If anyone loves Me, he will keep My word; and My Father will love him, and We will come to him and make Our home with him" (John 14:23). Christ would manifest Himself to anyone who loves Him.

True salvation produces a teachable heart in the believer. The desire to learn and change in response to the Word of God is the mark of a true disciple of Christ.

Simon: The Political Zealot

A few years ago, I preached a message to my congregation titled "The Deadly Dangers of Moralism" in which I outlined fifteen reasons that Christian political activism and lobbying efforts should not be the focus of Christian ministry. In the months that followed, several Christian leaders publicly criticized my teaching and suggested that I was undermining the efforts to moralize our country.

In the midst of those personal attacks, the Lord used a senior staff member for a high–ranking elected official in Washington to encourage me. "I'm a Christian," he said, "and I've heard your tape on moralism. There are many Christians on our staff, and I want you to know that our approach to politics has been transformed by your teaching. We had viewed our political opponents as the enemy, and completely missed the fact that the Lord sees them as our mission field."

That conversation reminds me of one of Jesus' lesser–known

apostles, Simon the Zealot (Luke 6:15). At one time, Simon was apparently a member of the Zealots, a well–known and widely feared outlaw political sect in the first century. They hated the Romans, and their goal was to overthrow the Imperial occupation of their land. They hoped Messiah would lead them in their revolt and would restore the kingdom to Israel. The Zealots were red–hot patriots, ready to die in an instant for what they believed in. Many were terrorists who concealed daggers under their garments and would assassinate Roman soldiers and politicians by stabbing them in the back.

Simon was one of those political hotheads, but somewhere along the line he became a genuine believer and was transformed. He worked side by side with the other apostles for the spread of the gospel and worshiped the Lord, even though He was not fulfilling the Messianic mission as Simon had once envisioned it. The fiery enthusiasm he formerly had for Israel was now expressed in his devotion to Christ.

> THE MAN WHO WAS ONCE WILLING TO KILL AND BE KILLED FOR A POLITICAL AGENDA HAD FOUND A MORE FRUITFUL CAUSE FOR WHICH TO GIVE HIS LIFE— THE PROCLAMATION OF SALVATION TO SINNERS OUT OF EVERY NATION, TONGUE, AND TRIBE.

Several early sources indicate that Simon took the gospel north and preached in the British Isles. There is no reliable record of what ultimately happened to him, but all accounts say he was killed for preaching the gospel. The man who was once willing to kill and be killed for a political agenda had found a more fruitful cause for which to give his life—the proclamation of salvation to sinners out of every nation, tongue, and tribe.

Well–intentioned but misinformed Christians may be urging you to devote your energies to political activism on a variety of moral issues. Before you leap into that arena, consider the example of Simon. He left his political passions behind for the sake of proclaiming the gospel, and modeled what the Christian's ultimate priority should be.

Delivered from Slavery

John Newton, an eighteenth–century Englishman, ran away to sea early in life and finally settled in Africa. In what seems to be a reversal of roles at the time, he came under the domination of a black woman. He lived off the crumbs from her table and supplemented his diet with wild yams he secretly dug out of the ground at night. His clothing was reduced to a single shirt, which he periodically washed in the ocean. Newton eventually escaped his slavery but exchanged it for another, living a debauched life among the natives.

God laid hold of him, however, through an African missionary. John Newton became a sea captain and later a minister of Jesus Christ.

JOHN NEWTON
RAN AWAY TO SEA
EARLY IN LIFE...
BECAME A SEA
CAPTAIN AND LATER
A MINISTER OF
JESUS CHRIST.

*I am not what I ought to be.
I am not what I wish to be.
I am not even what I hope to be.
But by the cross of Christ,
I am not what I was.*

JOHN NEWTON

He went on to write many great hymns, including the beloved "Amazing Grace." Ultimately, he became a pastor of a church in England, where he served until his death in 1807. His epitaph, which he himself wrote, reads:

John Newton, Clerk
Once an infidel and libertine,
A servant of slaves in Africa,
Was, by the rich mercy of our Lord and Saviour, Jesus Christ,
Preserved, restored, pardoned,
And appointed to preach the faith
He had long laboured to destroy.

John Newton's life was indeed wretched before he came to Christ. But after his conversion he wrote, "I am not what I ought to be. I am not what I wish to be. I am not even what I hope to be. But by the cross of Christ, I am not what I was."

Praise be to God, who takes our sinful lives and transforms them to His glory!

The Disciple's Prayer Life

True prayer for a disciple of Jesus Christ begins and ends with the glory of God (John 14:13). Prayer should be concerned primarily with who God is, what He wants, and how He can be glorified. Nineteenth–century pastor E. M. Bounds rightly said, "Prayer honors God; it dishonors self."

God is eager to lend His ear, His power, and His eternal blessing to the prayers of His children when their requests further His

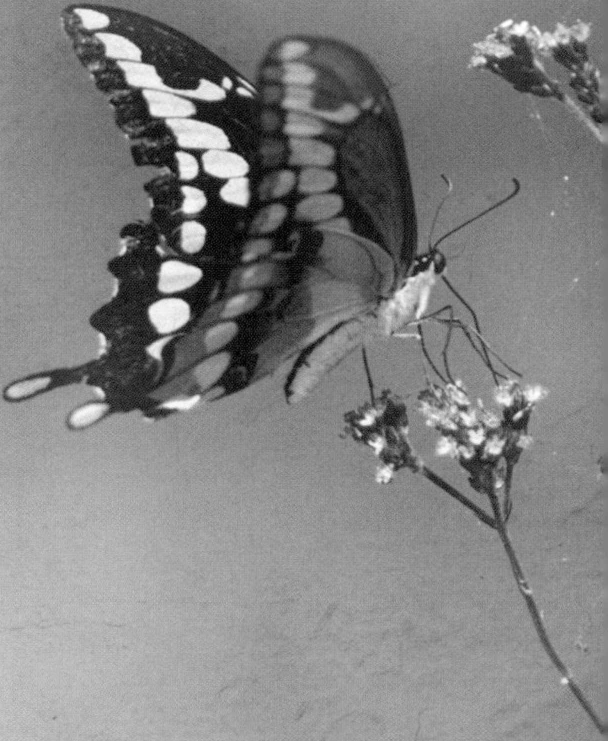

purpose and glory. "Therefore let us draw near with confidence to the throne of grace, so that we may receive mercy and find grace to help in time of need" (Hebrews 4:16).

*Praise be to God,
who takes our sinful lives
and transforms them
to His glory!*

THOSE WHO FAILED *to* FOLLOW

Judas Iscariot: Greed and Betrayal

For most of us, the name "Judas Iscariot" is synonymous with treachery and betrayal. Even superficial readers of the New Testament recognize Judas as the one who betrayed the Lord into the hands of those who crucified Him. While no one in his right mind would hold Judas forth as a spiritual example, his life contains a surprising warning for all of us.

Judas was an ordinary man like the other disciples. The Bible does not tell us how he came to follow Jesus, but he obviously followed Him willingly. He undoubtedly was like other Jews in the first century, eager for the Messiah to come. He was probably a young, patriotic Jew who hoped that Jesus would overthrow the Roman oppressors and restore the kingdom to Israel. With his political yearnings, Judas initially had plenty of reason to be attracted to Christ.

But political motivations are not a true basis for following Christ. Judas followed Jesus only to satisfy his own desires for selfish gain, worldly influence, and greed. He recognized Jesus' power, but he didn't want to bend his knee to Him. He wanted to use Jesus' power and influence to accomplish his own goals. When he didn't get what he wanted, he betrayed the Son of God for thirty silver coins (Matthew 26:14–16).

Judas' life illustrates the fundamental problem with calling people to faith in Christ so that He can meet their felt needs, fix their family problems, or give miraculous relief to financial difficulties. People who supposedly decide to follow Christ for those reasons will turn their backs on Him as soon as they don't get what they want. The call to follow Christ must always be grounded in submission to Him in repentant faith for salvation from sin—not to achieve some earthly benefit. Jesus said that His kingdom was not of this world (John 18:36).

Examine your heart and test your motives for following Christ. Do you desire intimacy with Him because of who He is and His rightful claim on your life? Or do you want Him at your beck and call to accomplish your own

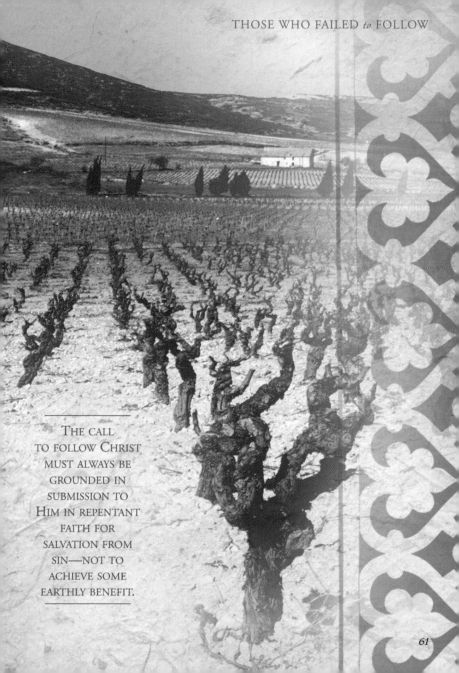

THE CALL
TO FOLLOW CHRIST
MUST ALWAYS BE
GROUNDED IN
SUBMISSION TO
HIM IN REPENTANT
FAITH FOR
SALVATION FROM
SIN—NOT TO
ACHIEVE SOME
EARTHLY BENEFIT.

selfish desires? Flee from Judas' selfish example, which always leads to betraying Christ, and follow Christ on His terms, to His glory.

Supernatural Defection

Many people are attracted to Christianity because they want miraculous healing, deliverance, and financial provision. They flock to teachers who promise them that Jesus will meet their needs if they have faith to believe Him for their personal miracle.

> FASCINATION WITH THE SUPERNATURAL IS NOT PROOF OF TRUE DISCIPLESHIP. IT MAY ONLY BE A THINLY VEILED ATTEMPT TO USE GOD TO FULFILL SELFISH DESIRES.

Similar people crowded Jesus during His ministry. They flocked around Him when He miraculously fed the multitudes (John 6:1–15), but left when He called for a spiritual commitment (John 6:60–66). They couldn't get miracles on their own terms, so they left Jesus behind.

Fascination with the supernatural is not proof of true discipleship. It may only be a thinly veiled attempt to use God to fulfill selfish desires. The shallow follower has no sense of the spiritual, lives only for today, and will defect when Christ does not fulfill all his or her earthly desires.

Confronting False Teachers

You undoubtedly know the uncomfortable feeling that comes from answering the door and finding two cult members on the other side who want to tell you about their religion. Many people have the misguided notion that you should avoid being controversial in your conversation with them, lest you somehow turn them away from the true gospel.

The Bible does tell us to be gentle when correcting those who are in opposition to the faith (2 Timothy 2:24–26). But a gentle spirit does not preclude clear correction. Jesus rebuked the Pharisees at length during His ministry (Matthew 23:1–36), and sometimes faithfulness will call us to rebuke false teachers as well.

I've done that on several occasions to those who have come to my door to talk to me about their cult. I tell them that I'm not interested in hearing what they teach and let them know what Jesus said about those who teach false doctrines. I also let them know that I'm happy to share the truth with them, but I don't want to hear their lies.

If you are frank with those involved in false religious systems, you'll plant a thought that they can't escape. That is much more powerful than letting such visitors think they have defeated you in a debate about biblical doctrine. You need to confront them. When you do, ask the Spirit of God to guide you. We need to call people away from false religious systems and, as it were, snatch them out of the fire (Jude 23).

Soldiers: Ignorant Mockery

The Roman soldiers who crucified Jesus went out of their way to humiliate Him before His death. Not satisfied with the physical torment they inflicted on him, they also mocked Him in blasphemous ways (Matthew 27:27–31). To them, Jesus was simply another condemned prisoner who they were free to abuse as much as they pleased—a prisoner who claimed to be some sort of king.

First, the soldiers stripped Him of His garment and draped Him with a scarlet robe. Scarlet was apparently the closest the soldiers could come to purple—the traditional color of royalty. Then they wove a crown of thorns and thrust it on His head, mimicking the wreath that Caesar wore on official occasions. They placed a reed in His right hand as if it were a monarch's scepter that symbolized authority and power. The low point of their ridicule came when they kneeled before Him and said, "Hail, King of the Jews!" spat on Him, and beat Him with their fists. Their actions all were designed to expose Jesus for the fraud He supposedly was.

The world is full of people today who are like those soldiers of old. Many people laugh at even the thought of Jesus, seeing Him as a joke. They simply don't know who they are callously rejecting. What do you do with people like that? Follow Jesus' example. "Father, forgive them, for they do not know what they are doing" (Luke 23:34). And God answered Jesus' prayer. When they saw how He died, only hours after they had mocked him, the Roman soldiers exclaimed, "Truly this was the Son of God!" (Matthew 27:54).

Don't give up on those who mock Christ when you share your faith. God is able to turn their hearts to saving faith in the most surprising ways.

> DON'T GIVE UP ON THOSE WHO MOCK CHRIST… GOD IS ABLE TO TURN THEIR HEARTS TO SAVING FAITH IN THE MOST SURPRISING WAYS.

Deathbed Attitudes

Jesus was crucified with two robbers. The Greek term used to identify the thieves indicates that they were cruel bandits who took pleasure in tormenting, abusing, and often even killing their victims.

You might think that the robbers would have been so preoccupied with their own fate and suffering that they would have ignored Jesus. Not so. They joined with the crowd in casting insults at Him (Matthew 27:44). We don't know why they hated Jesus. He certainly had done them no harm. Perhaps their wicked hearts somehow perceived His life as a righteous judgment on their sinfulness.

Yet before death came, one of those robbers turned on his fellow criminal and rebuked him for his insults (Luke 23:39–41). He then humbly asked Jesus to remember Him when He entered into His kingdom—a request Jesus gladly fulfilled (Luke 23:42–43).

The two robbers offer both hope and warning to us today.

TODAY IS THE DAY
OF SALVATION.
TODAY IS THE DAY
TO REPENT.

The repentant thief offers hope that it is never too late to turn to Christ. But the unrepentant thief warns us not to take salvation for granted. He was facing imminent death, had Jesus right before eyes, and saw another thief receive forgiveness. But Scripture seems to indicate that he died without repentance and entered into a Christless eternity.

If you haven't yet received Christ, don't assume that you'll turn to Him in the face of death. You may not have time to prepare for death, and even if you do, your heart may be too stubborn to seek Christ in your final moments. No, today is the day of salvation. Today is the day to repent.

Religious Hypocrisy

By far the most wicked of those who harassed Jesus at the cross were the Jewish religious leaders. They were the primary instigators of the crucifixion. They represented the entire religious leadership of Israel, which resolutely opposed Jesus and sought His destruction.

If any group of people should have known God's truth and recognized and received the Messiah, it was those men. Yet they not only opposed and condemned Jesus themselves, they

GOD IS SOVEREIGN
OVER EVEN THE
MOST WICKED MEN
AND THEIR MOST
WICKED ACTS.

also enticed the people to support them in their wicked rejection of Him (Matthew 27:20,41).

Those men had much to do with religion, but nothing to do with God (Romans 2:17–20; 10:2). But because they professed great knowledge of God and presumed that they were pleasing Him, they were the guiltiest of all who participated in Jesus' death—as Jesus Himself affirmed (John 19:11).

But in God's economy, their wickedness didn't have the final word. Before all eternity, God had planned to use their wicked devices to accomplish His plan to have Jesus die for sinners (Acts 2:23). God is sovereign over even the most wicked men and their most wicked acts. The leaders meant it for evil, but God meant it for good (Genesis 50:20).

THE COST *of* FOLLOWING

The Call to Persecution

My ministry has taken me throughout the world over the years, and I thank the Lord for the variety of places He's allowed me to visit. The lands of Russia particularly hold a special place in my heart. The pastors and leaders there have encouraged and challenged me with the depth of their commitment to Christ. I've spoken with many who have spent long years in prison, away from their families and their congregations, only because they were faithful to proclaim the saving gospel of Jesus Christ.

Few believers have suffered that kind of persecution in Western nations, and I'm convinced that the church is poorer as a result. If you examine the lives of the apostles after Jesus' resurrection, you'll find that each of them ultimately gave his life for the sake of the gospel. History records that all but one of them were killed for their testimony. Only John is said to have lived to old age, and even he was severely persecuted for Christ's sake, then exiled to the tiny island of Patmos.

The pastors in the lands of Russia are like the apostles. They have triumphed despite the obstacles they have faced. In the midst of great persecution at the hands of their government, they fulfilled the task of preaching the gospel and making disciples. Persecution of Christians is often the seed of true revival and church growth, no matter how difficult the circumstances may be.

> MANY OF US WILL NEVER TASTE THE KIND OF PERSECUTION THAT THE APOSTLES OR THE BROTHERS OVERSEAS HAVE KNOWN. BUT THE WILLINGNESS TO ENDURE SACRIFICE FOR THE SAKE OF CHRIST SHOULD NEVER BE FAR FROM OUR THINKING.

You don't have to seek persecution to prove your faithfulness to the gospel, but as a disciple of Jesus Christ, your heart should be willing to embrace sacrifice and persecution for His sake. Jesus said, "'A slave is not greater than his master.' If they persecuted Me, they will also persecute you" (John 15:20). The apostle Paul said, "All who desire to live godly in Christ Jesus will be persecuted" (2 Timothy 3:12).

Many of us will never taste the kind of persecution that the apostles or the brothers overseas have known. But the willingness to endure sacrifice for the sake of Christ should never be far from our thinking. No cost is too high in the service of the One who laid down His life to purchase our eternal salvation.

Discipleship in a Hostile Environment

I thank God that He placed me in a godly family. From my earliest days, I knew the godly instruction and discipline that comes from Christian parents. Their impact on my life cannot be measured; it is enough to say that I would not be the man I am today apart from their influence.

Some believers, of course, don't have that privilege. I routinely speak with people who face hostility to their Christian faith from a parent, spouse, or other loved one. Often, the hostility comes with a condescending attitude toward the Christian faith, as if Christianity were some old wives' tale not worthy of their consideration. Many young believers suffer great affliction at the hands of family members who reject their faith.

How should these precious believers respond to their difficulties? Some may try to argue with their loved ones, but heated discussions rarely produce any positive results. Others may retreat and find their faith badly shaken by the challenge. Is there a better way?

The best response to such hostility is to recognize that on a human level, the gospel is a foolish message. Jesus' apostles were deemed unsophisticated preachers whose teaching was beneath the elite. They were nobodies who often were denied a fair hearing for their message.

But that's all right. God's favorite instruments are nobodies, so that no man can boast before God (1 Corinthians 1:26–29). God chooses whom He chooses in order that He might receive the glory. He chooses weak instruments so that no one will attribute the power to human instruments rather than to God, who wields the instruments.

If you're a Christian in a hostile environment that seemingly

> IF YOU'RE A
> CHRISTIAN IN
> A HOSTILE
> ENVIRONMENT
> THAT SEEMINGLY
> RENDERS YOU
> WEAK...LET
> YOUR PASSION FOR
> CHRIST DRIVE
> YOUR LIFE...

renders you weak, look to the example of the apostles. Their influence was not rooted in their innate abilities or the perception of others. Their influence came from one thing and one thing only: the power of the message they preached. Let your passion for Christ drive your life, and trust God for the effect that has on those around you.

The Call to Self-Denial

The easy way is never the way of success. Great medical researchers risk exposure to deadly disease to save thousands of lives. Great musicians sacrifice their social lives to perfect their skills. Great athletes constantly train their bodies, denying themselves indulgences most people take for granted. Success comes at the price of a singular focus.

The life of John the Baptist illustrates that truth. His life could never be described as easy. He wore "a garment of camel's hair, and a leather belt about his waist; and his food was locusts and wild honey" (Matthew 3:4). He was God's messenger, but he didn't live, dress, or talk like the other religious leaders of the day.

John's lifestyle was a stern rebuke to the self–indulgent leaders of Israel. Both physically and symbolically he separated himself from their hypocritical religion and corrupt political systems. He was so consumed by God's calling that he was not attracted to the world's enticements.

Today, his lifestyle reminds us that worldly pleasures may not come to those who follow God's will completely and humbly. For many of us, self–denial will be the ultimate test of our devotion to God.

FOR MANY
OF US, SELF—DENIAL
WILL BE THE
ULTIMATE TEST OF
OUR DEVOTION
TO GOD.

The Call to Repentance

Several years ago, a nationally known preacher sent me a book he had written in which he redefined sin as nothing more than a poor self-image. The way to reach people, he said, is to bolster their self-esteem, not to make them think of themselves as sinful. There is no gospel in a message like that! Rather than bringing people to salvation, it confirms them in the self-condemning vanity of their own egos. How different that approach is from the Russian believers who all refer to their salvation as their "repenting."

The gospel is first of all a mandate for repentance from sin. Jesus said, "I have not come to call the righteous but sinners *to repentance*" (Luke 5:32; emphasis added). From the beginning of Jesus' ministry, the heart of His message was a call to repentance (Matthew 4:17). No one who refuses the call to repentance can be a true disciple of Jesus Christ.

The Disciple's Attitude toward Material Things

Every disciple of Christ should heed the words of J. H. Jowett. He said, "The real measure of our wealth is how much we would be worth if we lost all our money." He was right. Earthly riches or the lack of them has nothing to do with real wealth. Jesus plainly taught that the only treasure that matters is the treasure we lay up in heaven (Matthew 6:19–21).

If you want to take your spiritual temperature, look at your checkbook. Where are you investing your treasure? That is where your heart really is. God does not give us riches to hoard for ourselves, but to use for His glory. True enjoyment of our wealth comes not from possessing it, but from investing it as God intended—in things that count for eternity.

The real measure of our wealth
is how much we would be worth
if we lost all our money.

J. H. JOWETT

PROMISES *to* FOLLOWERS

The Value of "Insignificant" Gifts

No gift is too small when put into the Lord's hands. Jesus taught His disciples that lesson in Luke 21:1–4:

> "He looked up and saw the rich putting their gifts into the treasury, and He saw also a certain poor widow putting in two mites. So He said, 'Truly I say to you that this poor widow has put in more than all; for all these out of their abundance have put in offerings for God, but she out of her poverty put in all the livelihood that she had.'"

The poor person who gives everything he or she has is giving a greater gift than rich people who give much more out of their abundance. In God's economy, the sacrificial faithfulness of the giver, not the size of the gift, is the true measure of the gift's significance.

That's a difficult concept for the human mind to comprehend. It is not the greatness of the gift that counts, but rather the greatness of the God to whom it is given. He takes the sacrificial and seemingly insignificant gifts of His people who give faithfully, and promises to use them to accomplish monumental things.

The Value of Inconspicuous Service

Some people won't play in the band unless they can beat the big drum. Peter had that tendency. But not Andrew. He is never named as a participant in the big debates. He was more concerned about bringing people to Jesus than about who got the credit or who was in charge. He had little craving for honor.

Andrew is the very picture of all those who labor quietly in humble places, "not with eyeservice, as men–pleasers, but as slaves of Christ, doing the will of God from the heart" (Ephesians 6:6). He was one of those rare people who is willing to take the back seat and be in the place of support. He did not mind being hidden as long as the work was being done.

Many Christians today would do well to learn that lesson. The Lord values people like Andrew. They're the quiet men and women, laboring faithfully but inconspicuously, who accomplish the most for the Lord. They don't

THE QUIET
MEN AND WOMEN,
LABORING
FAITHFULLY BUT
INCONSPICUOUSLY…
ACCOMPLISH
THE MOST FOR
THE LORD.

receive much recognition, but they don't seek it. They only want to hear the Lord say, "Well done."

The Certainty of a Fruitful Life

The wonderful reality about following Christ is that it is so profoundly meaningful. Everything in life has eternal significance for the disciple of the eternal Son of God. Jesus promised His disciples, "He who abides in Me and I in him, he bears much fruit" (John 15:5).

Unlike an unbeliever, whose life has only a limited effect on others, the follower of Jesus Christ has a life that matters forever. When you share the gospel with someone who ends up receiving Christ, you have been part of an eternal transaction. Like the ripples in a pond when a rock is thrown in, your life ripples throughout all eternity with fruit born in time to the glory of God.

The Certainty of Answered Prayers

As Jesus was speaking to His disciples on the night before His crucifixion, He made a staggering promise to them. "You did not choose Me but I chose you, and appointed you that you would go and bear fruit, and that your fruit would remain, *so that whatever you ask of the Father in My name He may give to you* (John 15:16; emphasis added).

God answers the prayers of Jesus' true followers. To pray in Christ's name simply means to ask for what Jesus would want accomplished. The intent of such praying is not to ask for something so you can "spend it on your pleasures" (James 4:3). Instead, when your prayers are aligned with the desires of Jesus Christ, God will answer them. You can draw upon the infinite resources of God in prayer with the certainty that He will hear and answer if you are a follower of Christ.

> YOU CAN DRAW UPON THE INFINITE RESOURCES OF GOD IN PRAYER WITH THE CERTAINTY THAT HE WILL HEAR AND ANSWER IF YOU ARE A FOLLOWER OF CHRIST.

The Promise of Heaven

Jesus promised more than answered prayer to His troubled disciples on that night before His crucifixion. He also told them:

> "In My Father's house are many dwelling places; if it were not so, I would have told you; for I go to prepare a place for you. If I go and prepare a place for you, I will come again and receive you to Myself, that where I am, there you may be also" (John 14:2–3).

As a child, whenever I traveled away from home for very long, I thought the best thing I could possibly do was go back to my house. The warmth and love of home cannot be found anywhere else. Heaven is like that for you as a Christian. Going to heaven won't be like going into a giant palace where you have to be formal with people you don't know very well. When you go to heaven, it will be like going home.

WHEN YOU GO
TO HEAVEN,
IT WILL BE LIKE
GOING HOME.

The Promise of Christ's Presence

During World War II, a German ship picked up a missionary whose ship had been torpedoed. He was put in the hold, but the situation did not terrify him. When his friends asked him how he endured the night, he replied, "I began communing with the Lord, and remembered Psalm 121: 'My help comes from the Lord, who made heaven and earth. He will not allow your foot to slip; He who keeps you will not slumber. Behold, He who keeps Israel will neither slumber nor sleep.' So I said, 'Lord, there isn't really any use for both of us to stay awake tonight. If you are going to keep watch, I'll thank Thee for some sleep!'"

That missionary had a practical understanding of the Lord's presence. Jesus told His disciples, "Lo, I am with you always, even to the end of the age" (Matthew 28:20). No matter what happens in your Christian life, the Lord Himself is there with you, and He has the resources and power you need. Draw near to Him in believing prayer, and look at those troubling circumstances as great opportunities for God to display His faithfulness to you.

REFLECTIONS *on* FOLLOWING CHRIST

The Context of Discipleship

It was common, both in the Greek culture and the Jewish culture of Jesus' day, for a prominent rabbi or philosopher to attract students. Their teaching venue was not necessarily a classroom or an auditorium. Most were traveling instructors whose disciples simply followed them through the normal course of everyday life.

That is the kind of ministry Jesus maintained with His followers. He was an itinerant teacher. He simply went from place to place, and as He taught, He attracted people who followed His movements and listened to His teaching.

We get a picture of this in Luke 6:1: "Now it happened that He was passing through some grainfields on a Sabbath;

and His disciples were picking the heads of grain, rubbing them in their hands, and eating the grain." They were walking with Him, following Him from place to place as He taught, gleaning grain for food as they walked. For the apostles, ordinary life was the context of discipleship.

It's still the same for you today. Following Christ isn't rooted in spectacular events, juiced-up conferences, or continual mountaintop experiences. It's found in loving Him, obeying Him, thanking Him, and glorifying Him in the most mundane daily details of life. The apostle Paul said, "Whether, then, you eat or drink or whatever you do, do all to the glory of God" (1 Corinthians 10:31).

For the true disciple of Jesus Christ, every moment is packed with eternal significance, because all of life—even the smallest of details—is lived in His presence. Don't despise the routine of life, but find in the routine the platform on which you develop deep intimacy with the God of the universe who ordains each of your days.

What Are You Hungry For?

In John 6:51, Jesus said, "I am the living bread that came down out of heaven; if anyone eats of this bread, he will live forever." He was saying that a sinner may have eternal life by receiving Him personally into His life.

Jesus likened that exercise of faith to eating bread. You can sniff bread, squeeze it, and comment on how good it must be; but you won't benefit from it unless you eat it. Likewise, you won't receive any eternal benefit from Christ until by faith you receive Him into your life (John 1:12–13).

We Walk by Faith, Not by Sight

We can live life in one of two contrasting fashions. The approach that comes naturally to us is to live empirically— basing all our thoughts and actions on what we can see and experience. The other fashion, which does not come naturally to us, is to live by faith—basing life primarily and ultimately on what we cannot see or feel.

The apostle Paul said, "We walk by faith, not by sight" (2 Corinthians 5:7). The Christian has never seen God the Father, the Lord Jesus Christ, or the Holy Spirit. He can't see heaven or hell. He has never talked to any of the Spirit–led authors of Scripture. He cannot see the spiritual graces and virtues God gives.

> WE BASE OUR PRESENT LIVES AND FUTURE DESTINIES ON INVISIBLE REALITIES. IT HAS ALWAYS BEEN THAT WAY FOR THE TRUE FOLLOWERS OF GOD.

Even though none of those important aspects of Christianity is tangibly visible, as believers we are convinced by faith of their truthfulness and we live accordingly. We base our present lives and future destinies on invisible realities. It has always been that way for the true followers of God.

Those who have gone before us in this unseen faith have left behind footsteps for us to follow. My prayer for you is that you would leave your own footsteps for someone else in this marvelous walk of faith that we call the Christian life.

Well Done, Good and Faithful Slave

When the apostle Paul approached death at the end of his ministry, he told his beloved disciple Timothy, "I have fought the good fight, I have finished the course, I have kept the faith" (2 Timothy 4:7). When he entered the presence of his Lord, Paul no doubt heard the comforting words, "Well done, good and faithful slave . . . enter into the joy of your master" (Matthew 25:21).

It should be the goal of all servants of Christ to hear those words from their Master. To aim at anything less is unworthy of the Lord who has graciously called us and given us all the spiritual resources we need to serve Him honorably and always glorify His name (2 Peter 1:3–4).

LEAVE YOUR OWN
FOOTSTEPS FOR
SOMEONE ELSE IN
THIS MARVELOUS
WALK OF FAITH
THAT WE CALL THE
CHRISTIAN LIFE.

Balancing Truth and Love

The epistle of 2 John is one of the lesser-known portions of Scripture, yet it illustrates a key concept in living the Christian life. Throughout the epistle, John repeatedly connects the concepts of love and truth.

Many people are imbalanced in their approach to the Christian life. They place too much emphasis on the love side of the fulcrum. For them, truth is turned into error, clothed in a shallow, tolerant sentimentality. That is a poor substitute for genuine love.

Others, however, have all their theological ducks in a row and know their doctrine, but are unloving and self-exalting. They are left with truth as cold facts, stifling and unattractive. Their lack of love cripples the power of the truth they profess to revere.

The truly godly person must cultivate both virtues in equal proportions. If you pursue anything in the spiritual realm, pursue a balance of truth and love. Know the truth, and uphold it in love (Ephesians 4:15).

The Bible, Discipleship, and Ministry

One of the greatest problems in the church today is ignorance. Some professing Christians have gone to church for years and yet they know next to nothing about the Bible. God doesn't tolerate that. Paul said, "Study and be eager and do your utmost to present yourself to God approved" (2 Timothy 2:15, AMP).

If you are thinking about going into some type of Christian ministry that requires teaching or evangelizing, you need to be trained. You can't just say, "I'm ready; I'm going to go out into the world and tell everyone what I know about Christ." That won't work. You will run out of things to say if you're not adequately prepared.

People ask me why I spent so much time in school before I became a pastor. Without that schooling I would not have been equipped to teach God's Word. Every year I spent in school, and every hour I now spend in study, contributes to my ministry. We need to know God's Word before we can share it with others.

> WE NEED TO KNOW GOD'S WORD BEFORE WE CAN SHARE IT WITH OTHERS.

If you have desires for ministry, may the Lord give you grace and blessing as you seek to do His will. But don't rush into His service without knowing the Scriptures and sound theology. It takes time and effort, but it's worth it.

The Crossroads of Your Destiny

As we've seen throughout this book, what you do with Jesus Christ involves far more than raising your hand or walking an aisle at a church meeting. Your response to Christ is a

JESUS HIMSELF STANDS AT THE CROSSROADS OF YOUR DESTINY AND DEMANDS A DELIBERATE CHOICE OF LIFE OR DEATH, HEAVEN OR HELL.

once–for–all verdict with ongoing implications and eternal consequences.

Jesus said, "Enter through the narrow gate; for the gate is wide and the way is broad that leads to destruction, and there are many who enter through it. For the gate is small and the way is narrow that leads to life, and there are few who find it" (Matthew 7:13–14). In that statement, Jesus was calling people

to put their faith in Him for eternal salvation and to follow Him as Lord.

Jesus Himself stands at the crossroads of your destiny and demands a deliberate choice of life or death, heaven or hell. The Lord requires that each person choose between following the world on the easy, well–traveled road or following Him on the difficult road.

*It seems to be the will of God
that I must shortly leave you.
You are now to be left fatherless,
which I hope will be an inducement
to you all, to seek a Father who
will never fail you . . . Trust in God,
and you need not fear.*

JONATHAN EDWARDS

The choices are clear–cut. He demands a decision. We all are at the crossroads, and each individual must choose which way he or she will go. Have you repented of your sins and committed your life to Christ? If you have, rejoice—He will be faithful to complete the work that He has begun in your life, no matter what your present difficulties may be (Philippians 1:6). If you're still standing outside the gate, don't delay any longer. Come to Christ and enter into eternal life.

Those You Leave Behind

When Jonathan Edwards, a great theologian from the 18th century, was facing an early death at the age of 54, he told his children, "It seems to be the will of God that I must shortly leave you. You are now to be left fatherless, which I hope will be an inducement to you all, to seek a Father who will never fail you." His final words were, "Trust in God, and you need not fear" (Iain Murray, *Jonathan Edwards: A New Biography*, 441).

Some Christians feel mixed emotions when they contemplate going to heaven because they understandably are concerned about what will happen to the loved ones they leave behind. Jonathan Edwards gives us a beautiful example to follow. Point those loved ones to Christ and rest in the assurance that just as He cared for you during your earthly life, so He will also care for them and lead them in the right paths in your absence. You can entrust your beloved ones to Christ with the same confidence in His goodness as you entrusted your own eternal soul to His gracious care. Commit them to Him, then rest in Him.

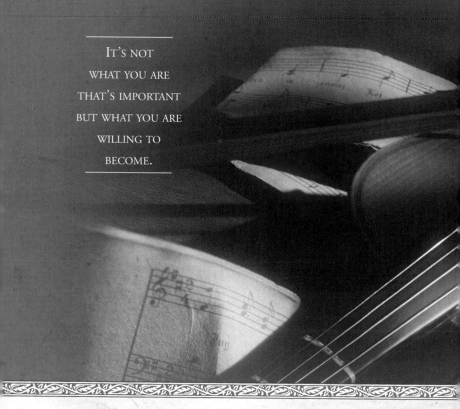

IT'S NOT
WHAT YOU ARE
THAT'S IMPORTANT
BUT WHAT YOU ARE
WILLING TO
BECOME.

What About You?

The story is told of a great violinist who announced he would give a concert using an unusually expensive violin. On the designated night, violin lovers packed the hall to hear the instrument played. The violinist came out on stage and gave an exquisite performance, climaxed by a thunderous ovation from the appreciative crowd. He bowed to acknowledge the cheers,

then suddenly threw the instrument to the floor, stomped it to pieces, and walked offstage. The audience was horrified.

A few moments later, the stage manager came out and said to the stunned crowd, "Ladies and gentlemen, the violin that was just destroyed was only a twenty–dollar violin. The maestro will now return to play on the advertised instrument." He did so, and few could tell the difference.

Beloved friend, it isn't primarily the violin that makes the music; it's the violinist. Most of us are twenty–dollar violins at best, but in the Master's hands we can make beautiful music. God uses ordinary people with a variety of strengths and weaknesses. It's not what you are that's important but what you are willing to become. Christ's earthly life was filled with the work of transforming common men and women into uncommon messengers of His gospel. He can do a similar work in your life as well.

Running the Race

I can still remember the first time I ran the half–mile for my high school track team. I usually ran the 100–yard dash, which requires only a quick burst of speed. So I started out well in the half–mile; in fact I led the pack for the first 100 yards or so. But my legs were soon wobbly, I was completely out of breath, and I collapsed at the finish line, dead last.

THE CHRISTIAN RACE IS A MARATHON, NOT A SPRINT.

That's the way many believers live the Christian life. They start out fast, but, undisciplined and adrift spiritually, they soon encounter obstacles or impediments, slow down, give up, or just collapse. The Christian race is a marathon, not a sprint. To win a marathon, you must be disciplined to endure weariness and exhaustion. The same is true in the Christian life.

The writer of Hebrews says, "Let us run with endurance the race that is set before us" (12:1). He's calling us to run the race with the desire to win—in other words, to live life with excellence so that we honor Christ in all we do.

Nothing is more disturbing than to see Christians who have little desire to win. I believe that lack of desire is a basic problem with many believers. They are content simply to be saved and to wait to go to heaven. But that's unacceptable for a follower of Christ.

If you claim allegiance to Jesus Christ as your Lord, you need to strive for as much excellence as you can in every endeavor. If you're a Sunday school teacher, be the most excellent teacher you can be. If you lead a Bible study, lead your flock with excellence. If you're a homemaker, make your home as excellent as it can be. When you're at your job, do the most excellent work you can.

> IF YOU CLAIM ALLEGIANCE TO JESUS CHRIST AS YOUR LORD, YOU NEED TO STRIVE FOR AS MUCH EXCELLENCE AS YOU CAN IN EVERY ENDEAVOR.

That's the only way to live the Christian life. It takes discipline, but we must demand excellence of ourselves and run the race to win.

Enjoying the Fruits of Victory

No one would run a marathon without some expectation of reward. And the same is true of the race of faith—if you don't have something to look forward to at the end of it, you'll likely never start it, let alone finish it. So the writer of Hebrews encourages us with the outcome of Jesus' faith: "who for the joy set before Him endured the cross, despising the shame, and has sat down at the right hand of the throne of God" (12:2).

The reward that awaited Him at the end of His earthly ministry motivated Jesus to leave the glories of heaven and endure what He did. Two aspects of that reward motivated Jesus: "the joy set before Him" and sitting "down at the right hand of the throne of God." Jesus ran the race of faith for the joy of exaltation. In His high–priestly prayer He said to His Father, "I glorified You on the earth, having accomplished the work which You have given Me to do. Now, Father, glorify Me together with Yourself, with the glory which I had with You before the world was" (John 17:4–5). Jesus glorified God on earth by displaying the Father's attributes and completing His Father's will.

We run for the same reason Jesus did, and we achieve victory in the same way. We run for the joy of exaltation that God promises will be ours if we glorify Him on earth. By following our Lord's example, we glorify God by allowing His attributes to shine through us and by obeying His will in everything we do.

But we can also experience joy now as we anticipate the heavenly reward of our faithful

WE RUN
FOR THE SAME
REASON JESUS DID,
AND WE ACHIEVE
VICTORY IN THE
SAME WAY.

WE GLORIFY
GOD BY ALLOWING
HIS ATTRIBUTES TO
SHINE THROUGH US
AND BY OBEYING
HIS WILL IN
EVERYTHING
WE DO.

service. The reward at the end thus becomes our motivation to forget "what lies behind and [reach] forward to what lies ahead," pressing on "toward the goal for the prize of the upward call of God in Christ Jesus" (Philippians 3:13–14).

When we get to heaven, we can join the twenty–four elders in casting our "crowns before the throne, saying, 'Worthy are You, our Lord and our God, to receive glory and honor and power'" (Revelation 4:10–11).

As we run the race of the Christian life and follow in the footsteps of the great men and women of faith, we can joyfully look forward to receiving the crown of righteousness, which we will cast at our Lord's feet as proof of our eternal love for Him.

Will you be there?

FOR MORE INFORMATION

Grace to You is the Bible–teaching media ministry of John MacArthur. In addition to producing the worldwide *Grace to You* and *Grace to You Weekend* radio broadcasts, the ministry distributes more than two dozen books by John MacArthur and has produced more than thirteen million audiocassette lessons since 1969.

For more details about John MacArthur and all his Bible–teaching resources, contact us at 800-55-GRACE or www.gty.org.